Days and Times

BY KATHY THORNBOROUGH • ILLUSTRATIONS BY KATHLEEN PETELINSEK

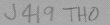

The Child's World®

PUBLISHED by The Child's World®
1980 Lookout Drive • Mankato, MN 56003-1705
800-599-READ • www.childsworld.com

ACKNOWLEDGMENTS
The Child's World®: Mary Berendes, Publishing Director
The Design Lab: Design
Jody Jensen Shaffer: Editing

PHOTO CREDITS
© Angela940/iStock.com: back cover, 3; Ansis Klucis/Shutterstock.com: 20; Ase/Shutterstock.com: 7; Bildagentur Zoonar GmbH/Shutterstock.com: 5; Franck-Boston/iStock.com: back cover, 14; GeorgeDolgikh/iStock.com: 12; Huansheng Xu/Shutterstock.com: 22; John Gomez/Shutterstock.com: 8; khuruzero/Shutterstock.com: 15; Luke Thomas/Shutterstock.com: 4; northallertonman/Shutterstock.com: 21; Pablo Hidalgo/Shutterstock.com: 18; photosync/Shutterstock.com: cover, 1, 6; Samarets1984/Shutterstock.com: 23; Serhiy Kobyakov/Shutterstock.com: 11; Tang Yan Song/Shutterstock.com: 19; Thinglass/Shutterstock.com: 16; tntemerson/iStock.com: 9; Trifonov_Evgeniy Trifonov_Evgeniy/iStock.com: 10; Viacheslav Krylov/Shutterstock.com: 13; YuryZap/Shutterstock.com: 17

ISBN 9781626873162
LCCN 2014934491

PRINTED in the United States of America
Mankato, MN
July, 2014
PA02216

A SPECIAL THANKS TO OUR ADVISERS:

As a member of a deaf family that spans four generations, Kim Bianco Majeri lives, works, and plays amongst the deaf community.

Carmine L. Vozzolo is an educator of children who are deaf and hard of hearing, as well as their families.

J419 THO

JAN 2015

NOTE TO PARENTS AND EDUCATORS:

The understanding of any language begins with the acquisition of vocabulary, whether the language is spoken or manual. The books in the Talking Hands series provide readers, both young and old, with a first introduction to basic American Sign Language signs. Combining close photocues and simple, but detailed, line illustrations, children and adults alike can begin the process of learning American Sign Language. Let these books be an introduction to the world of American Sign Language. Most languages have regional dialects and multiple ways of expressing the same thought. This is also true for sign language. We have attempted to use the most common version of the signs for the words in this series. As with any language, the best way to learn is to be taught in person by a frequent user. It is our hope that this series will pique your interest in sign language.

Time

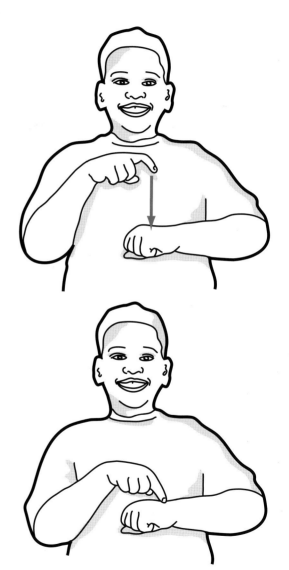

Some people wear a watch to tell the time.

Tap your wrist a few times as if you are tapping a watch.

3

Second

Spell S-E-C with your fingers.

The red hand on this clock shows the seconds. There are 60 seconds in one minute.

Minute

The long hand on this clock shows the minutes. There are 60 minutes in one hour.

Twist your right hand forward as if it were the minute hand on a clock.

5

Hour

Make the "L" shape with your right hand. Touch the pinky-side of your right hand to your open left hand. Move your right hand in a circle until you end up in the starting position.

There are 24 hours in one day.

Morning

Place your flat left hand inside your right elbow. Move your flat right hand toward your face.

7

Afternoon

Make both of your hands flat. Angle your right arm out and away from your body. Touch your left index finger to your right elbow.

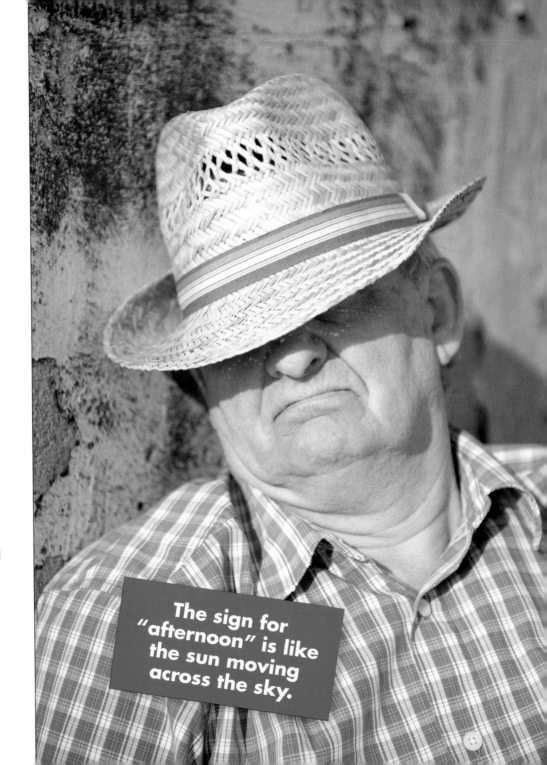

The sign for "afternoon" is like the sun moving across the sky.

Night

The sign for "night" is like the sun going down.

Make both of your hands flat.
Put your right wrist over your left.
Bend your right wrist.

9

Day

Make the "L" shape with your right hand. Go from pointing straight up to touching your left arm.

There are 365 days in one year.

Be sure to see page 24 to learn how to sign all the letters.

Early

Spell E-A-R-L-Y with your fingers as you move your hand clockwise.

11

Late

Bend your right arm at your elbow.
Push your flat right hand backward—
as if you are pushing
something behind you.

Later

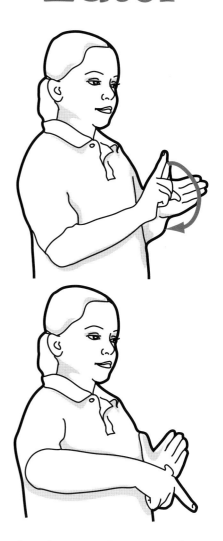

Make the "L" shape with your right hand. Your right thumb should touch your left hand. Twist your right hand until it points downward.

13

Week

Make the "1" sign with your right hand. Slide it off your left hand.

14

monday

tuesday

wednesday

thursday

friday

saturday

sunday

> There are 7 days in one week.

Sunday

Face your hands forward. Move both hands in, up, and out in a circle.

Many people consider Sunday the first day of the week.

Monday

Make the "M" shape with your right hand, facing toward you. Move your hand in circles.

The word "Monday" comes from an old word meaning "moon day."

16

Tuesday

Some people think Tuesdays are unlucky.

Make the "T" shape with your right hand facing toward you. Move your hand in circles.

Wednesday

Make the "W" shape with your right hand facing toward you. Move your hand in circles.

Wednesday is the middle of the work and school week.

Thursday

The word "Thursday" comes from an old word meaning "Thor's Day."

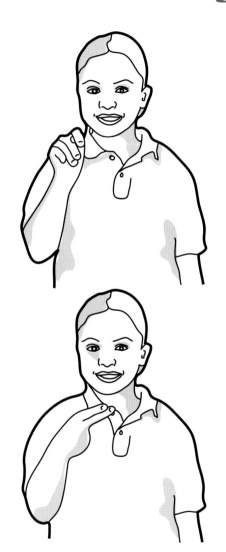

Make the "T" shape with your right hand. Then the "H" shape. Repeat.

Friday

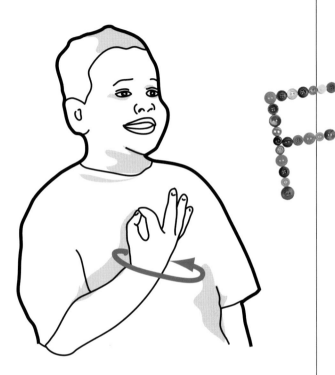

Make the "F" shape with your right hand facing toward you. Move your hand in circles.

Many people like Friday. It is the beginning of the weekend.

Saturday

Saturday is named after Saturn.

Make the "S" shape with your right hand facing toward you. Move your hand in circles.

Month

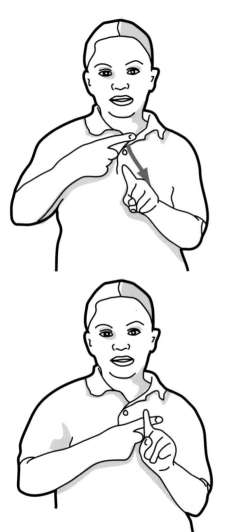

Both hands make the "1" sign.
Your left hand points up and stays still.
Your right index finger points left
and slides down once.

22

1 JANUARY						
S	M	T	W	T	F	S
			1	2	3	4
5	6	7	8	9	10	11
12	13	14	15	16	17	18
19	20	21	22	23	24	25
26	27	28	29	30	31	

There are 12 months in one year.

Year

January
Sun	Mon	Tue	Wed	Thu	Fri	Sat
		1	2	3	4
5	6	7	8	9	10	11
12	13	14	15	16	17	18
19	20	21	22	23	24	25
26	27	28	29	30	31	

February
Sun	Mon	Tue	Wed	Thu	Fri	Sat
						1
2	3	4	5	6	7	8
9	10	11	12	13	14	15
16	17	18	19	20	21	22
23	24	25	26	27	28	

March
Sun	Mon	Tue	Wed	Thu	Fri	Sat
						1
2	3	4	5	6	7	8
9	10	11	12	13	14	15
16	17	18	19	20	21	22
23	24	25	26	27	28	29
30	31					

April
Sun	Mon	Tue	Wed	Thu	Fri	Sat
		1	2	3	4	5
6	7	8	9	10	11	12
13	14	15	16	17	18	19
20	21	22	23	24	25	26
27	28	29	30			

May
Sun	Mon	Tue	Wed	Thu	Fri	Sat
				1	2	3
4	5	6	7	8	9	10
11	12	13	14	15	16	17
18	19	20	21	22	23	24
25	26	27	28	29	30	31

June
Sun	Mon	Tue	Wed	Thu	Fri	Sat
1	2	3	4	5	6	7
8	9	10	11	12	13	14
15	16	17	18	19	20	21
22	23	24	25	26	27	28
29	30					

July
Sun	Mon	Tue	Wed	Thu	Fri	Sat
		1	2	3	4	5
6	7	8	9	10	11	12
13	14	15	16	17	18	19
20	21	22	23	24	25	26
27	28	29	30	31		

August
Sun	Mon	Tue	Wed	Thu	Fri	Sat
					1	2
3	4	5	6	7	8	9
10	11	12	13	14	15	16
17	18	19	20	21	22	23
24	25	26	27	28	29	30
31						

September
Sun	Mon	Tue	Wed	Thu	Fri	Sat
	1	2	3	4	5	6
7	8	9	10	11	12	13
14	15	16	17	18	19	20
21	22	23	24	25	26	27
28	29	30				

October
Sun	Mon	Tue	Wed	Thu	Fri	Sat
			1	2	3	4
5	6	7	8	9	10	11
12	13	14	15	16	17	18
19	20	21	22	23	24	25
26	27	28	29	30	31	

November
Sun	Mon	Tue	Wed	Thu	Fri	Sat
						1
2	3	4	5	6	7	8
9	10	11	12	13	14	15
16	17	18	19	20	21	22
23	24	25	26	27	28	29
30						

December
Sun	Mon	Tue	Wed	Thu	Fri	Sat
	1	2	3	4	5	6
7	8	9	10	11	12	13
14	15	16	17	18	19	20
21	22	23	24	25	26	27
28	29	30	31			

Make the "S" shape with both hands. Your left hand stays still while your right hand moves forward in a circle until it ends up at the starting position.

It takes one year for Earth to go all the way around the Sun.

A SPECIAL THANK YOU!

A special thank you to our models from the Program for Children Who are Deaf and Hard of Hearing at the Alexander Graham Bell Elementary School in Chicago, Illinois.

Alina's favorite things to do are art, soccer, and swimming. DJ is her brother!

Dareous likes football. His favorite team is the Detroit Lions. He also likes to play video games.

DJ loves playing the harmonica and video games. Alina is his sister!